As new doors of opportunity open before you, I encourage you to walk through them. Be bold in pursuit of your passion. Be smart in the ways you execute your plans. Be creative in the journey so that your light shines bright. Be courageous in your daily endeavors and be confident that you are designing your own life as it was intended.

Be.Inspired. Be.Empowered.
Touch the Sky!

Sincerely Yours,

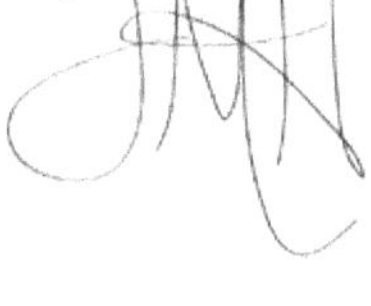

www.juliemholloway.com
www.twitter.com/jmhcre8ive

✪ Get that Fearless Faith! ✪

www.ingramcontent.com/pod-product-compliance
Lightning Source LLC
Chambersburg PA
CBHW070924180526
45168CB00005B/2139
9781511986007